HIP-HOP HEADLINERS

5
1/16
1/21

JAY-Z

Gareth Stevens
Publishing

By Roman P. Nacerous

Please visit our Web site, www.garethstevens.com. For a free color catalog of all our high-quality books, call toll free 1-800-542-2595 or fax 1-877-542-2596.

Library of Congress Cataloging-in-Publication Data

Nacerous, Roman P.
  Jay-Z / Roman P. Nacerous.
    p. cm. — (Hip-hop headliners)
  Includes index.
  ISBN 978-1-4339-4796-4 (library binding)
  ISBN 978-1-4339-4797-1 (pbk.)
  ISBN 978-1-4339-4798-8 (6-pack)
  1. Jay-Z, 1969—Juvenile literature. 2. Rap musicians—United States—Biography—
Juvenile literature. I. Title.
  ML3930.J38N33 2010
  782.421649092—dc22
  [B]
                                2010023237

First Edition

Published in 2011 by
Gareth Stevens Publishing
111 East 14th Street, Suite 349
New York, NY 10003

Copyright © 2011 Gareth Stevens Publishing

Designer: Haley W. Harasymiw
Editor: Therese Shea

Photo credits: Cover, pp. 2–32 (background) Shutterstock.com; cover (Jay-Z), p. 1 Rolf Klatt/WireImage; p. 5 Kevork Djansezian/Getty Images; p. 7 Brad Barket/Getty Images; p. 9 Robert Mora/Getty Images; p. 11 Frank Micelotta/ABC/Image Direct; p. 13 Matthew Peyton/Getty Images; pp. 15, 17, 29 Frank Micelotta/Getty Images; p. 19 Scott Gries/ Getty Images; p. 21 Lary Busacca/Getty Images for NARAS; p. 23 Ian Gavan/Getty Images; p. 25 Christopher Polk/Getty Images; p. 27 Al Bello/Getty Images.

Printed in the United States of America

CPSIA compliance information: Batch #CW11GS: For further information contact Gareth Stevens, New York, New York at 1-800-542-2595.

Contents

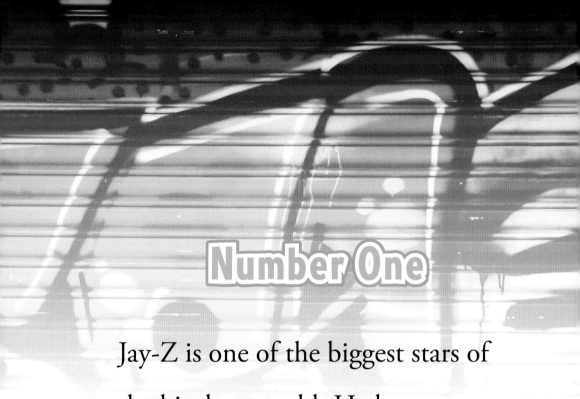

Number One

Jay-Z is one of the biggest stars of the hip-hop world. He has more number-one albums than any other artist!

5

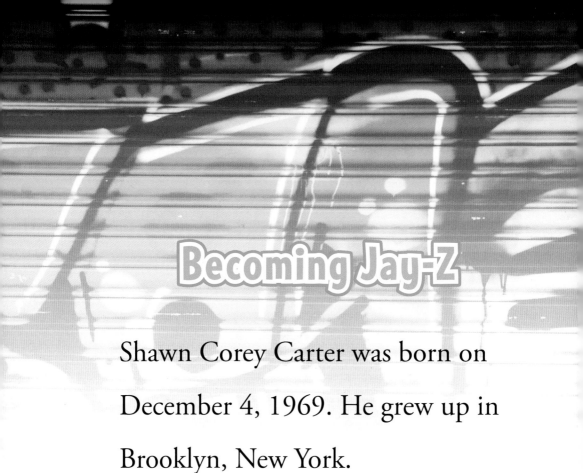

Becoming Jay-Z

Shawn Corey Carter was born on December 4, 1969. He grew up in Brooklyn, New York.

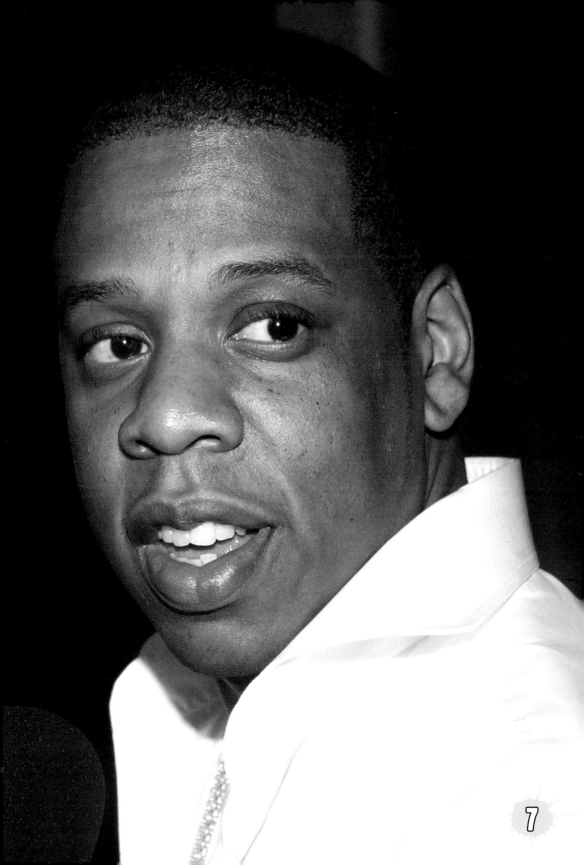

Shawn lived in a poor neighborhood. He began rapping at a young age. People called him "Jazzy." He changed this name to "Jay-Z."

Jay-Z started his own music business. His first album came out in 1996. It was called *Reasonable Doubt*.

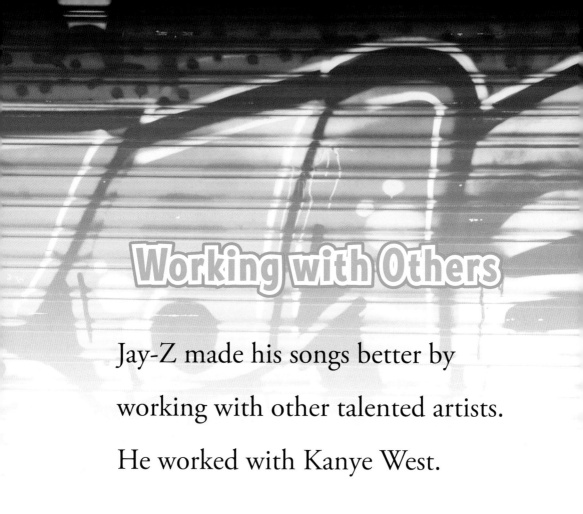

Working with Others

Jay-Z made his songs better by
working with other talented artists.
He worked with Kanye West.

Kanye West

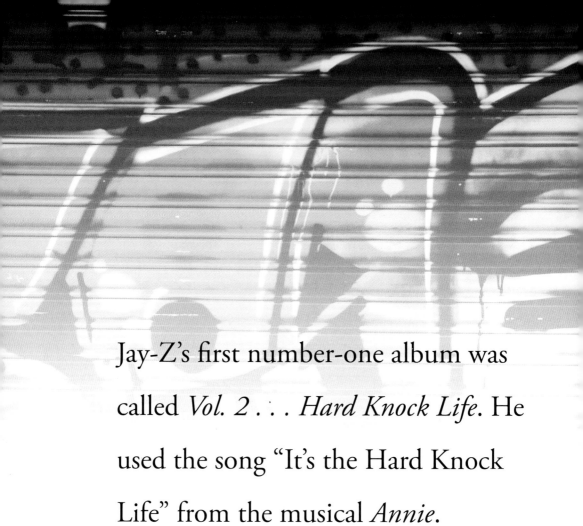

Jay-Z's first number-one album was called *Vol. 2 . . . Hard Knock Life*. He used the song "It's the Hard Knock Life" from the musical *Annie*.

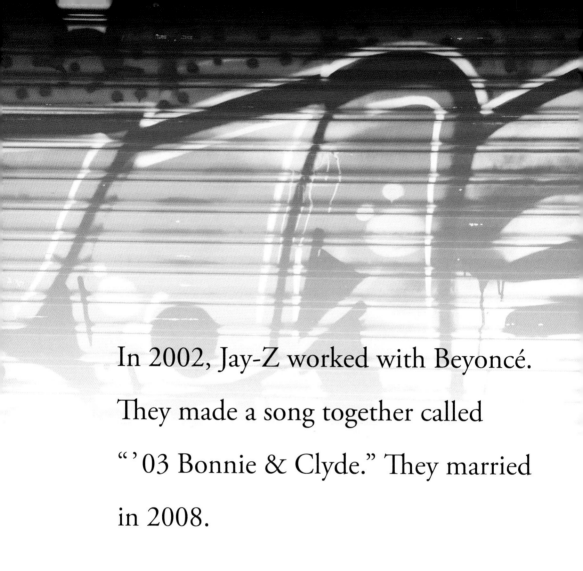

In 2002, Jay-Z worked with Beyoncé.
They made a song together called
"'03 Bonnie & Clyde." They married
in 2008.

Beyoncé

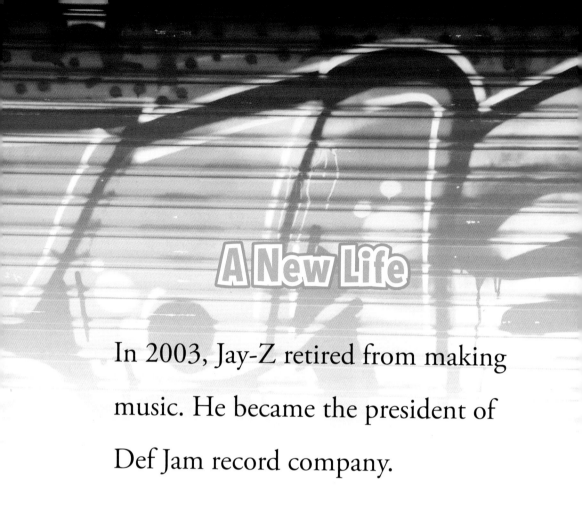

A New Life

In 2003, Jay-Z retired from making
music. He became the president of
Def Jam record company.

19

At Def Jam, Jay-Z helped young hip-hop artists. Rihanna was one of Jay-Z's new stars.

Rihanna

21

Back to Music

After a few years, Jay-Z decided to make his own music again. His next three albums were number one on the charts!

Jay-Z loves New York City. He wrote the song "Empire State of Mind" to tell how he feels. He sang it with Alicia Keys.

Alicia Keys

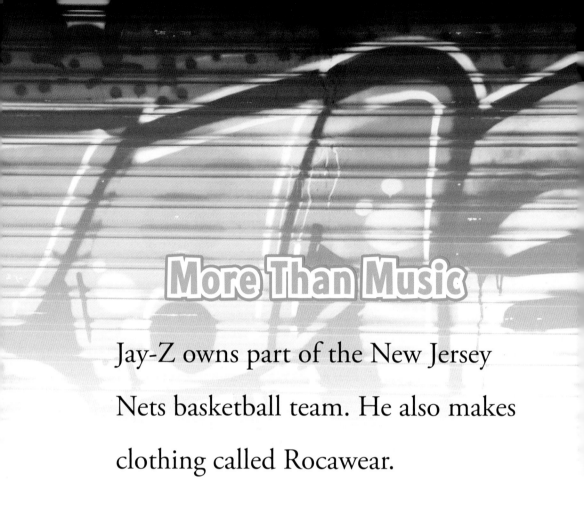

More Than Music

Jay-Z owns part of the New Jersey
Nets basketball team. He also makes
clothing called Rocawear.

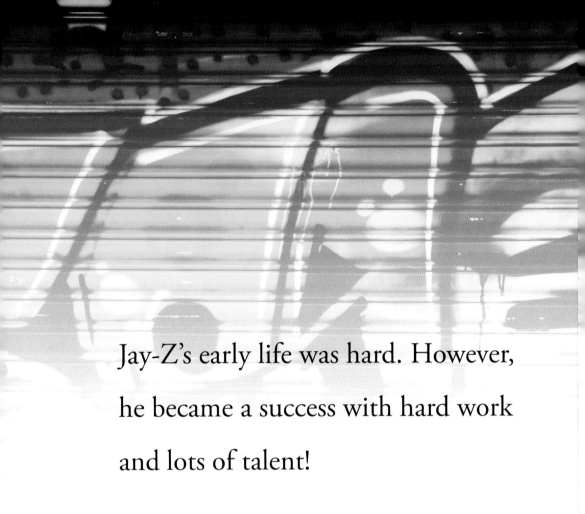

Jay-Z's early life was hard. However, he became a success with hard work and lots of talent!

Timeline

1969   Shawn Corey Carter is born in
Brooklyn, New York.

1996   Jay-Z's first album comes out.

1998   *Vol. 2 . . . Hard Knock Life*
becomes a number-one album.

2003   Jay-Z retires from making albums.
He becomes head of Def Jam.

2006   Jay-Z begins making his own
albums again.

2008   Jay-Z marries Beyoncé.

2009   Jay-Z's "Empire State of Mind"
becomes a number-one hit.

For More Information

Books:

Abrams, Dennis. *Jay-Z.* New York, NY: Chelsea House, 2008.

Barnes, Geoffrey. *Jay-Z.* Broomall, PA: Mason Crest Publishers, 2007.

Hillstrom, Laurie Collier. *Jay-Z.* Detroit, MI: Lucent Books, 2010.

Web Sites:

Jay-Z

www.mtv.com/music/artist/jay_z/artist.jhtml#biographyEnd

Jay-Z

www.jay-z.com

Glossary

charts: lists of songs or albums that have sold well

musical: a movie or play that tells a story with singing and often dancing

record company: a business that produces and sells music

retire: to leave a job

talented: gifted

Index